30 DAY BEAUTIFUL BOTTOM

GW01003521

BY DEBORAH COX AND JULIE DAVIS

DESIGNED BY JON DEWEY

PHOTOS BY MARTIN JACKSON

BANTAM BOOKS
TORONTO · NEW YORK · LONDON · SYDNEY

Before starting any new exercise or diet program, it's always best to have a medical checkup. This is a must if you have any serious medical conditions or if you are taking medication. Call your doctor before you begin.

30 DAYS TO A BEAUTIFUL BOTTOM
A Bantam Book / August 1982

All rights reserved.
Copyright © 1982 by Cloverdale Press, Inc.

ISBN 0-553-01472-2

Published simultaneously in the United States and Canada

Bantam Books are published by Bantam Books, Inc. Its trademark, consisting of the words "Bantam Books" and the portrayal of a rooster is Registered in U.S. Patent and Trademark Office and in other countries. Marca Registrada. Bantam Books, Inc., 666 Fifth Avenue, New York, New York 10103.

PRINTED IN THE UNITED STATES OF AMERICA

0 9 8 7 6 5 4 3 2

*T*ABLE OF CONTENTS

THE BARE FACTS 4
An introduction.

1. GETTING INTO GEAR 9
The who, what, when, where, and why
of exercise.

2. Act I: THE SUPER SEVEN 13
Seven high-powered bottom beautifiers
plus advanced variations.

3. ACT II: FREESTYLE DANCING 31
A fun aerobic exercise plus advice from
four fitness pros.

4. ACT III: THE BEAUTIFUL BOTTOM 45
DIET
A fresh approach to food.

5. FASHION SAVVY 53
How to look thinner *today*.

6. Q & A 59
A Potpourri of Information.

THE BARE FACTS:

An introduction

It sneaks up on you slowly and quietly. At first, you don't realize what's happening. You look over your shoulder—no, nothing out of the ordinary, you say. But your favorite pants do seem a bit tight. A loved one passes a teasing comment. You laugh, too. Then one day, the bare facts surface, almost by accident. You never meant to take out that tape measure! But you did, and there's no turning back. Call it the pear predicament or secretary spread, the fact is you're the victim of . . . fanny flab.

That first awareness — whether it's a sudden rear view of yourself in a full-length mirror, pants that refuse to be zipped, or a wicked yellow tape measure—is a shocker. But now there's a great way to fight back.

The answer to fanny flab is a no-nonsense, easy-to-follow plan that will give you a more beautiful bottom with results that start to show in just 30 days — you'll exercise just six days a week for five weeks (Sundays are free).

The plan is a three-act play: the Super Seven, a group of high-powered exercises that zero in on the hips and buttocks, and Freestyle Dancing, an aerobic activity that's fun to do and requires no equipment — you don't even have to leave your bedroom; and the Beautiful Bottom Diet, a new approach to weight control.

Have some doubts? Think that maybe exercise isn't for you? Well, it is. Exercise is for everyone. To see just how easy it is to begin, try the two exercises that follow. Bottoms up!

*T*WO START-UP EXERCISES YOU CAN DO NOW ... DO ANYTIME

STAND CORRECTED

Unless your mother drilled you on posture every day of your youth, your stance may be less than perfect. But the problem is easy enough to solve:

1. Pull your shoulders back to take the curve out of your spine.

2. Tuck your seat under by contracting the buttock muscles and tilting your pelvis (your hipbones) forward. Glamorous women still lead with their hips when they walk.

Do this seat muscle contraction whenever you can — these muscles can be squeezed and firmed even when you're lying in bed.

☆ This exercise is also good for the woman who wants to add roundness to a *flat* fanny.

SIT UPS

We've all heard about "secretary spread." Well, the truth is this phenomenon marches right up the corporate ladder, affecting assistants and executives alike. Whether your desk is in the boardroom or the mailroom, you may develop secretary spread unless you sit up, take notice and:

1. Sit slightly forward in your chair.

2. Press your pelvis forward, your stomach and bosom up. Sit tall, with your back straight. You should aim to sit on the upper part of your seat and feel the muscles in your thighs working to support your weight.

This position may feel odd at first, since you are probably used to collapsing on the broadest part of your seat and lower back, but you will adjust quickly. Note: The lower back should be pressed forward *with* your pelvis, not *against* the back of your chair.

REMEMBER

Sitting is better than lying down—
Standing is better than sitting down—
Walking is better than standing!

1. GETTING INTO GEAR

TAKE STOCK OF YOURSELF

The first step you take toward a more beautiful bottom may be the hardest, but it's a must. So if you haven't taken your current hip measurement yet, do it now. You have to know where you are at the start to fully appreciate the great results you're going to be seeing in only a few short weeks. Your eyes really can't distinguish each lost inch, but the tape measure can. Make sure to always measure yourself at the same point (i.e., six inches below the waist). Seeing that number drop will give you the incentive you need, week by week, to challenge yourself further.

MAKE A PROMISE TO YOURSELF

For any plan to be effective, you have to give it your all — an all-out effort to stick to your exercise strategy and to a sound diet. Reinforce your willpower by envisioning your goal: plant a picture of your new shape in your mind and promise to work to make it real.

Regardless of your bone structure, you can have a more beautiful bottom by toning your muscles — your shape is determined by their firmness and by the smoothness of your skin.

Just imagine how fabulous you will look after your first 30 days!

Before starting any new exercise or diet program, it's always best to have a medical checkup. This is a must if you have any serious medical conditions or if you are taking medication. Call your doctor before you begin.

*G*ET YOURSELF GOING

Have a few questions about how to begin? Arm yourself with these answers:

WHO?   Everyone! No one is immune to a sagging derrière. The good news? Everyone can benefit from exercise. The rewards are a trimmer, happier you, a sexier, healthier you, with more vitality and drive than you ever imagined — yes, even after a long day's work.

WHAT?   A no-frills set of seven exercises of varying repetitions and a dance period to get your heart and circulation racing. Reading through the exercises might seem an exercise in itself now, but you'll find that they take less time to do than to read. And the more you exercise, the more exercise your body will be able to handle. Rather than tire you out, the exercises will rev you up!

WHEN? Six days a week — Sunday was meant to be a day of rest, right? Bright and early is best — before you have a chance to make excuses. You'll work up a healthy sweat, so plan to shower *after*. If you work at home, try exercise instead of a heavy lunch. Before dinner is another possibility (exercise reduces the appetite).

WHERE? Pick out a spot you like: near a vase of flowers, a favorite poster or a picture window. Certainly be within earshot of your radio, cassette player, or stereo: music is a great boon to sagging spirits. Choose music with a lively tempo.

WHY? For a more beautiful body and a fabulous feeling of confidence. Diet alone isn't enough — losing fat is important, but good muscle tone is what makes you most attractive.

Here's how . . .

2. ACT 1: THE SUPER SEVEN

These exercises really work at developing your seat muscles (yes, there are muscles back there, the gluteal muscles). The exercises require stamina and perseverance, but you will find that the more you exercise, the more you want to exercise. What a bonus!

ON YOUR MARK

- Wear a sports bra if your bosom is larger than an A cup. You'll feel more comfortable if you do.

- Wear comfortable clothing: a leotard, a T-shirt, or maybe nothing more than comfy socks (good for the circulation). Don't worry about uniforms or expensive gear.

- Exercise on a comfortable surface; when the word "mat" is used (i.e. lie flat on your mat), that means an exercise mat, but it could be a rug, or two fluffy towels or a blanket—a bare floor is too hard.

- Turn on your favorite music.

*G*ET SET

- Proper breathing is a must. When you inhale, expand your tummy to take in as much air as you can. Hold the breath for three seconds, then slowly exhale, drawing in your tummy to get out as much air as you can. Continue this type of breathing throughout your workout.

- Warming up muscles is another must-do. After taking three good breaths, jog lightly in place for one minute (count to 60 slowly). Then do 10 fast jumping jacks or 20 jumps in place.

*G*O:

Here are the exercises. Do as many of the repetitions as you can. Beginners may not be able to do all of them, but try. Bear in mind that most of us just don't push ourselves hard enough.

☆ Each exercise is followed by an advanced variation. When the basic exercises get too easy, move on to these.

FANNY ROLL

Repetitions: 10, building up to 25

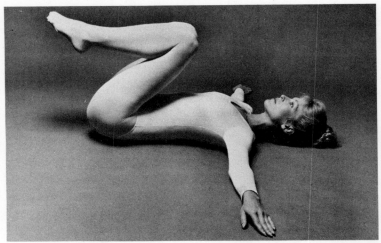

1. *Lie flat on your mat. Bend your knees and draw them into your chest. Stretch your arms out to the sides, at the level of your shoulders.*

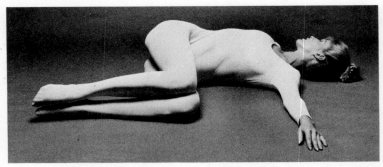

2. *Inhale. Keeping your shoulders firmly on the floor, slowly roll your hips to the right, bringing your knees as close to the floor as possible, and simultaneously turn your head to the left. Exhale and return to center. Without stopping, inhale and reverse: your hips roll to the left, your head to the right. Exhale and return to the center.*

You have just completed one full repetition.

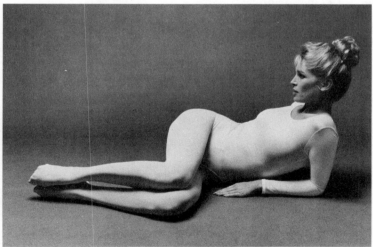

Advanced variation: *Prop your upper torso on your el-
bows. Your head stays centered while your hips roll right-
center-left-center, etc. Do the repetitions in double time—that
means twice as fast.*

PELVIC LIFT
Repetitions: 2, building up to 5

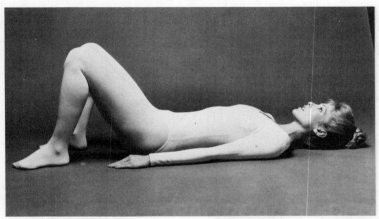

1. *Still lying flat, bring your arms down to your sides, palms down. Bend your knees and place your feet flat on the floor, about 12 inches apart.*

2. *Inhale and tighten the muscles in your buttocks as you slowly raise your seat off the floor. Push up the lower back, the middle back, and the upper back until you are supported by your shoulder blades and until your thighs are parallel to the floor. Hold 10 seconds.*

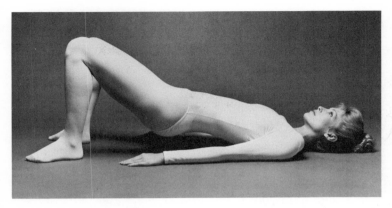

3. *Exhale and slowly roll down in reverse order: first touch down the upper back, then the middle back, then the lower back. Feel each vertebra in your spine uncurl, then roll down your hips. You have just completed one full repetition.*

Advanced variation: *During the up phase of each repetition, keep the thighs in line with each other and extend first the right calf to straighten the right leg. Hold this position for one second, then return the foot to the floor. Repeat the movement with the left calf, then roll your spine down.*

REAR LEG RAISES
Repetitions: 10 on each leg, building up to 50

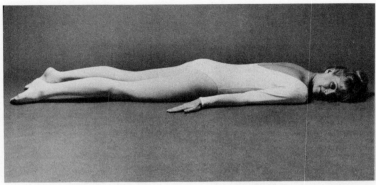

1. *Turn onto your stomach and place your arms at your sides, palms down. Rest either cheek on your mat, and open your legs about 6 inches. Contract the muscles in your buttocks and inhale.*

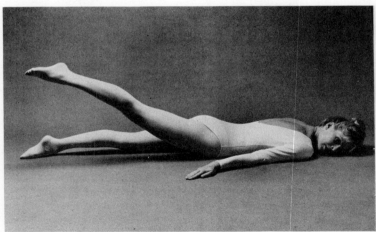

2. *With toes pointed, lift your right leg 6 inches off the floor. Hold this position for one second, then lower leg to the floor. Keep your hipbones on the mat at all times—that is more important than how high you lift the leg. Do all the reps on the right leg, then repeat them with the left.*

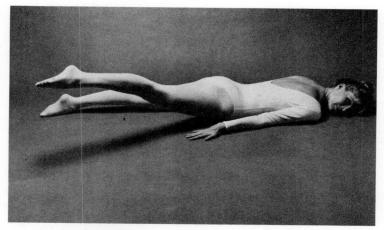

Advanced variation: *During the up phase of each rep, swing the leg out as far as possible. Hold the position for one second, then bring it back to center and lower it to the floor. Do the leg swings carefully and with control—no jerking.*

FLUTTER KICKS
Repetitions: 50 on each leg, building up to 100

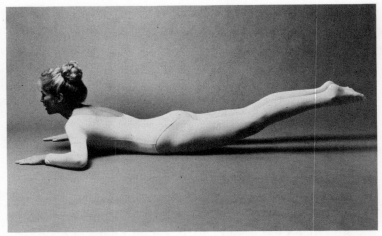

1. *Bend arms and place palms flat at shoulder level. Press palms and hipbones into the mat and lift both legs 6 inches off the floor. Breathing steadily, contract the muscles in your buttocks and flutter-kick legs just as you would if you were swimming. Again, do not lift hips off the mat.*

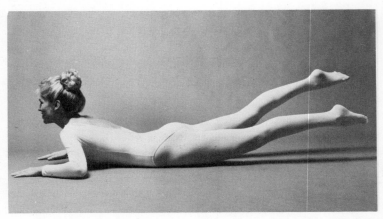

2. *Your legs should bob continuously: right-left-right-left, etc., and should not touch the floor during the exercise.*

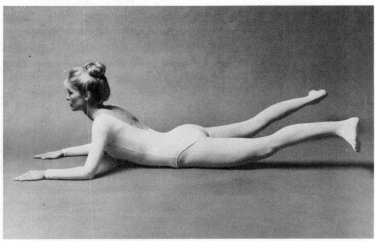

Advanced variation: *Scissor kicks. Instead of kicking up and down, kick in and out. Start with toes turned out, the left heel under the right heel. Both legs kick out to their respective sides and kick in with the left heel over the right heel, etc.*

KNEELING KICKS

Repetitions: 25 on each leg, building up to 50

1. *Bring yourself up on all fours, hands shoulder-width apart, knees 12 inches apart. Straighten your right leg behind you and raise it 12 inches off the floor.*

2. *Breathing steadily, bob the right leg up 25 times. Work as quickly as possible, never letting the leg touch the floor between bobs. Repeat the exercise with the left leg.*

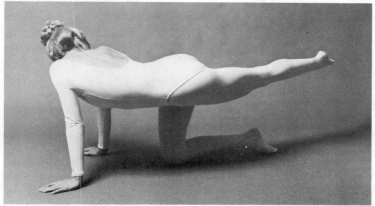

Advanced variation: *Start in the same position, right leg raised 12 inches. Simultaneously swing the right leg out as far as possible; twist at the waist and look over your right shoulder. Swing your body back to center and, without stopping, swing your right leg across to the left and twist your waist to look over your left shoulder. Return to center and you've completed one repetition. Keep count, but keep the movement continuous. Repeat with the left leg, which swings out to the left, then to the right.*

ARCHED KICKS
Repetitions: 10 on each leg, building up to 25

1. *Known in primitive circles as "donkey" kicks, these get the whole body moving. Still on all fours, inhale and curl your back, bringing your forehead toward your knees. Bring the right knee up to touch your forehead.*

2. Exhale, tighten seat muscles, and put your body in reverse: arch your back, lifting your head high, and extend the right leg behind you toward the ceiling. Bend your knee slightly to protect from strain—this exercise is also fast and continuous. Without stopping, inhale and draw the right knee and your forehead back together and continue with the next kick.

Do these as quickly as you can without jerking. Remember to tighten the muscles in your buttocks on the lift.

Advanced variation: *Maintain good form and increase speed as you build up to 50 reps on each leg.*

THE HINGE

Repetitions: 5, building up to 15

1. *Raise your torso until you are on your knees, your arms at your sides, palms lightly touching the outsides of your thighs.*

2. *Inhale. Keeping your back, torso, and thighs in one long, straight line, squeeze the muscles in your buttocks as tightly as you can and lean back. The tighter you tense the seat muscles, the more control you will have, and the farther back you'll be able to go. Hold five seconds. Exhale and return to the starting position. You have just completed one full repetition.*

Advanced variation: *Work at leaning farther back and holding for 10 seconds.*

3. ACT II: FREESTYLE DANCING

Aerobic exercise conditions the heart and the entire cardiovascular system, improves circulation, and can even reduce your heart rate.

So why dance, you wonder. Isn't running still *the* aerobic activity? There's no doubt that running is a high-intensity, high-calorie-burning exercise. But the truth is that many people find it boring, no fun at all, and painful to boot (even after reaching what runners call their natural "high").

Dancing, however, is always fun and exciting, a very physical activity that just doesn't feel like work, but which more than works off fat. Dancing is every bit an aerobic exercise. (*Aerobic* refers to the constant intake of oxygen during high-powered exercise. Oxygen is used by the body to burn fat reserves for fuel.)

Why freestyle dance? So that you can really let yourself go. Remember Jill Clayburgh's impromptu dance at the start of the film *An Unmarried Woman?* With hubby and daughter packed off for the day, she danced from room to room completely uninhibited. Now it is your turn to stage your most exotic performances.

Yes, there are special records and tapes with regimented aerobic dance programs, but they aren't necessary. Who wants to listen to instructions while dancing? This part of your attack on fanny flab is to be fun! Let your fantasies soar.

Make dancing a part of your workout. As soon as you have finished the Super Seven, switch to a very fast-paced record and shake, rattle, and roll to your heart's content. It's as easy as that!

Start with 10 minutes—that's 10 minutes without stopping, 10 minutes of huffing and puffing! Gradually work up to 30 minutes or more—perfect practice for an evening of dancing on the town.

*P*RACTICAL GUIDELINES AND AMAZING FACTS:

1. Start slowly, especially if you're out of practice. No need to rush into that half-hour goal. Your heart and lungs need to be strengthened little by little over a period of time. As you clock your minutes, week after week, you will become progressively stronger and able to handle more activity without feeling any strain.

2. Increase your workout time on a steady, consistent basis. It takes 20 minutes of aerobics in each daily session to improve the cardiovascular system. And once you attain that goal, don't rest on your laurels. The longer your workouts, the more fat you burn off.

Once the dance segment of your workout tops 30 minutes, more amazing changes may occur. You may successfully raise your metabolic rate, the speed with which your body burns calories. You may burn more calories per minute—not just when you are exercising, but all the time. That adds up to even more flab lost . . . to a more beautiful you all over.

3. For variety, consider other aerobic activities: biking (at home on a stationary bike is great —and private), swimming, skiing, rowing, walking—at four or five miles an hour—and, yes, running.

4. Always cool down after your daily workout. You want to gradually bring down your heart rate, just as you gradually raised it by running in place and doing jumping jacks at the start of the session.

Rather than collapse on the nearest bed, run in place for a full minute, slowing your pace at 15-second intervals. Then lie down on your exercise mat and practice deep breathing for another minute, taking in as much air as you can. Relax fully.

Cooling down this way enables you to get on with your day, in a positive, productive mood. Go for it!

EXERCISE PROGRESSION CHART

Exercise	Week 1	Week 2	Week 3	Week 4	Week 5
Fanny Roll	10 reps	10 reps	15 reps	20 reps	25 reps
Pelvic Lift	2 reps	3 reps	4 reps	5 reps	5 reps
Rear Leg Raises	10 reps each leg	20 reps each leg	30 reps each leg	40 reps each leg	50 reps each leg
Flutter Kicks	50 reps each leg	65 reps each leg	75 reps each leg	90 reps each leg	100 reps each leg
Kneeling Kicks	25 reps each leg	30 reps each leg	35 reps each leg	40 reps each leg	50 reps each leg
Arched Kicks	10 reps each leg	15 reps each leg	20 reps each leg	20 reps each leg	25 reps each leg
The Hinge	5 reps	10 reps	10 reps	15 reps	15 reps
Freestyle Dancing	10 min.	10 min.	15 min.	15 min.	20 min.

ADVANCED PROGRESSION CHART

Exercise	Week 6	Week 7	Week 8	Week 9	Week 10
Fanny Roll	10 reps	10 reps	15 reps	20 reps	25 reps
Pelvic Lift	5 reps	5 reps	7 reps	7 reps	10 reps
Rear Leg Raises	50 reps each leg	50 reps each leg	50 reps each leg	50 reps each leg	50 reps each leg
Flutter Kicks	50 reps each leg	65 reps each leg	75 reps each leg	90 reps each leg	100 reps each leg
Kneeling Kicks	25 reps each leg	30 reps each leg	35 reps each leg	40 reps each leg	50 reps each leg
Arched Kicks	30 reps each leg	35 reps each leg	40 reps each leg	45 reps each leg	50 reps each leg
The Hinge	15 reps	15 reps	15 reps	15 reps	15 reps
Freestyle Dancing	20 min.	25 min.	25 min.	30 min.	30 min.

ADVANCED LEVEL II

Do all the repetitions listed under Week 10 using ankle weights. See page 61 for a description of their use.

THE PROS SPEAK OUT

Four fitness experts offer their ideas:

Doris Boorstyn, director of the Yoga Studios of New York and yoga instructor at Hunter College, recommends the *asana*, or yoga position, known as *The Locust:*

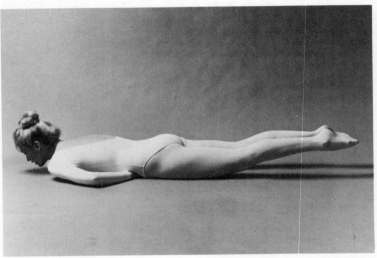

1. *Lie flat on your exercise mat, chin to the floor, legs straight. Make a fist with each hand and place them under your pelvis.*

2. *Inhale. Press down with your fists, exhale, and thrust your legs straight up, as high as possible. Hold this position for five seconds. Slowly lower your legs. Repeat three times.*

    Note: *If thrusting both legs at once is too difficult, first lift the right leg, hold, and release. Repeat the exercise with the left leg, then try both legs together.*

       Ellen Rubich, a dancer and faculty member at the Manhattan Ballet School, feels that ballet lessons on a regular basis are an excellent way to firm, trim, and beautify the entire body. Especially good for tightening the seat muscles are the classical ballet warm-ups at the barre. One of the best warm-ups is known as *dégagé:*

At home, use a secure doorknob in place of the barre for support. To start with your right leg, grasp the doorknob with your left hand. Slowly lift the right leg straight up in front of you, toes pointed, by tightening the seat and tummy muscles. Keep the rest of your body in a straight line–don't let your back sway. Slowly lower the leg, always using control. Repeat five times, then turn and grasp the knob with your right hand to work the left leg.

Note: At first, you might only be able to lift either leg only a few inches off the floor. That's fine. In time, as you practice, your legs will lift higher, up to hip level, parallel to the floor.

John Helion, a physical education instructor at Columbia University, suggests a variation of the rear leg raise to work the gluteal muscles:

Standing Rear Leg Lifts: *Stand a few inches from a wall and place the palms of your hands flat against it, at the level of your shoulders. Slowly lift your right leg behind you, as high as you can without bending it. Hold for three seconds and lower leg. Do 10 lifts with the right leg, then repeat the exercise using the left leg.*

Jeff Nayer, a prominent weightlifter and owner of New York's Rivereast Health Club, believes in weight training to develop muscle tone. He suggests squats and lunges, two exercises which, using weights, work together on gluteal (buttock) muscles.

Squats. *Stand with your legs about two feet apart and, using both hands, hold a dumbbell or barbell across the back of your shoulders. (Start with 10 pounds, build to 20 or more)*

Without bending your back, squat down until your thighs are just parallel to the floor–no lower. Tighten stomach muscles to help you return to a standing position. Start with a set of 20 repetitions, aim for three sets of 20. Beginners may do the squats "free-hand" (without using any weights).

<u>Lunges</u>. *Stand with your legs about a foot apart and hold a 10- or 15-pound weight bar across your shoulders. Lunge your right foot forward and press into this leg until the thigh is parallel to the floor and makes a right angle with the right calf. The left leg is straight behind you, foot flexed. Feel the stretch in the left calf. Straighten the right leg and repeat the lunge with the left foot forward. Start with a set of 10 repetitions, alternating right-left, right-left. Aim for three sets of 10. Beginners may use a broomstick instead of the weight bar.*

4. ACT III: THE BEAUTIFUL BOTTOM DIET

One beauty of exercise is the way it can change your perspective about food. Diet plans that don't call for exercise workouts are often ineffective. By a mysterious and wonderful process, a well-exercised body has little craving for sweets. After just a week of exercise, you won't want food as much because your brain stops sending out as many of those signals that send you to the fridge!

To experience this phenomenon, eat normally during your first week on the Beautiful Bottom program. Concentrate on the Super Seven and Freestyle Dancing. And notice how much less time you spend thinking about food.

Then make a four-week commitment to serious yet sound dieting. Think of that picture of the new you you planted in your mind and the promise you made to work to make it come true. Start the Beautiful Bottom Diet by reorganizing your nutritional priorities.

Most American diets look like this:

22%	complex carbohydrates
12%	protein
42%	fat
24%	sugar

Your revamped American diet will look like this:

48%	complex carbohydrates
30%	protein
12%	fat
10%	sugar

The **Beautiful Bottom Diet** stresses for weight loss, sound nutrition with increased fitness and good health. It is the new American approach to eating. The B.B. Diet counts portions rather than calories—no need to carry those charts around anymore. It is strict—so you don't have to make a lot of choices (the less you have to think about food the better).

Make up your daily meals from the selections in each category. Follow the portion guidelines *exactly*.

CARBOHYDRATES

Have every day:
1 large potato or 1 large banana (for potassium)

4 ounces of orange or grapefruit juice or ½ grapefruit or one tomato (for Vitamin C)

2 slices of whole-wheat bread, preferably from stone-ground flour (for fiber)

Plus choose:
1 cup of any vegetable
1 cup of or 1 piece of fruit

PROTEIN

**Choose 2
every day:**

3 ounces of chicken, turkey, veal, or lean meat— n.v.f. (*no visible fat*)

6 ounces of any shellfish

5 ounces of any fish except salmon and trout (they are too fatty)

2 eggs

8 ounces of low-fat (1%) cottage cheese

16 ounces of skim milk

FATS

**Choose 1
every day:**

1 ounce of nuts (weighed without the shell)

1¼ tablespoons of oil, preferably cold-pressed safflower or sunflower

1½ tablespoons of mayonnaise

1½ ounces of any cheese

1½ tablespoons of butter or margarine

Note: Always check with your doctor before starting a new diet. This is especially important if you must restrict your intake of salt or cholesterol.

SUGGESTIONS TO GET YOU STARTED

1. Make up at least four small meals from the allowed portions. Six mini-meals are better yet.

2. This diet calls for a minimum of kitchen time. Eat vegetables raw whenever you can. If you must cook them, steam them, never boil them.

3. Broil or bake fish, poultry, and meats; never fry.

4. Do not have red meat more than twice a week. Do not have eggs more than three times a week.

5. Try making your own whole-wheat bread (stone-ground flour is available at health-food stores—a good place to buy vitamins, too). If, for convenience, you mix the dough in a food processor, be sure to do the final kneading yourself, to tone upper arms.

6. Use mustard, soy sauce, hickory salt, and spices instead of gravy, sauces, mayo, and butter. Limit ketchup to one tablespoon a day.

7. Limit your use of diet dressings (use fresh pepper, herbs, and unusual vinegars from a gourmet shop), diet sodas (try club soda, or the new Italian mineral waters, with lime), and sugar substitutes.

8. Talk about dieting as little as possible. Even your best friends can turn out to be less than supportive. Concentrate on your goals and dream up private rewards.

9. After four weeks, if you are faithfully following the exercise progression chart and starting the advanced variations of the exercises, you may add one carbohydrate or one protein portion to your daily diet.

10. Remember your goal of a beautiful bottom in 30 days. You're on your way!

THE BEAUTIFUL BOTTOM DIET

SAMPLE MENUS

DAY I	Breakfast	4 ounces of orange juice 2 slices of whole-wheat bread 4 ounces of cottage cheese (½ portion)
	Lunch	6 ounces of cold cooked shrimp with lemon juice 1 cup of broccoli and cauliflower rosettes
	Midafternoon	4 ounces of cottage cheese (½ portion)
	Evening	3 ounces of broiled chicken 1 baked potato with butter (limit 1½ tablespoons) 1 cup of grapes

DAY II	Breakfast	Blender drink: mix 1 raw egg, 8 ounces of skim milk, 1 banana, 3 ice cubes, a dash of vanilla, cinnamon, and nutmeg
	Lunch	Roast beef sandwich: 3 ounces of lean meat on 2 slices of whole-wheat bread
	Midafternoon	1 pear and 1½ ounces of Cheddar cheese
	Evening	5 ounces of broiled bluefish 1 cup of lettuce and 1 tomato
DAY III	Breakfast	2 scrambled eggs on 2 slices of whole-wheat toast
	Lunch	8 ounces of cottage cheese with 1 cup of mixed berries
	Midafternoon	1 ounce of walnuts, freshly shelled
	Evening	½ grapefruit 5-ounce broiled veal chop (bone represents 2 ounces) 1 cup of steamed carrots with cinnamon 1 baked potato

5. FASHION SAVVY

You can start to look thinner the day you start exercising by using a bit of fashion savvy to create the illusion of a beautiful bottom.

$\mathcal{S}$OME GENERAL GUIDELINES:

- Avoid prints, expecially bold ones—they're just not very sophisticated, regardless of your weight; avoid all stripes (yes, even thin, vertical ones).

- Avoid clingy fabrics, like thin polyester knits, as well as stiff, bulky fabrics like tweeds and cable-stitch knits.

- Color-coordinated tops and bottoms give a sleek, classic appearance: a bright red silk shirt and skirt make a great look.

- Minimize fussiness—select simple styles, classic jewelry, not ethnic looks. Less is thinner!

- Start off correctly with the best-fitting undergarments you can afford.

NOW THE SPECIFICS:

The overall watchword is proportion. Compensate for wide hips by emphasizing your shoulders. Select fabrics with fullness. Wear blouses with full, Victorian collars.

Choose sweaters and jackets with solid shoulder padding or puffed or pleated sleeves. You can buy shoulder pads to attach to clothes you already own. Use Velcro, a fabric adhesive, to secure the pads.

Choose cowlneck sweaters that add dimension, not turtlenecks that make you look like their namesake.

Avoid clingy lycra and jersey type fabrics that lie close to the skin and make your upper torso look even more out of proportion to the hips.

Avoid sleeveless tops that break the smooth neck and shoulder line you want to emphasize. Instead, for dressy looks choose strapless tops or dresses or those with an off-the-shoulder treatment: bare shoulders take attention away from hips—and no look is more sensual.

If you have a nice waistline, be sure to accent this slimness with a belt—not one that is too wide or fussy. A simple, solid color leather or cotton sash, carefully wrapped, is a super look. Wide shoulders, narrow waist, ample hips ... the perfect Sophia Loren hourglass shape!

Definitely do not hide a good waistline under hip-length tunics or blousons or tent dresses—save that for Omar of the desert. (Note: a good waistline is any waistline at least 8 inches smaller than your hip measurement. Yes, time for that tape measure again!)

If your waistline isn't perfect, you should still avoid baggy dressing. Aim for a neat, tailored look. Most important: finding the proper size, even if that means another trip to the dressing room with try-ons.

On choosing skirts. Prevailing advice suggests an A-line skirt to hide wide hips, but a more important consideration has to do with fullness. That often means spending a few extra dollars. Cheap clothes cost less because they are made with a minimum of material and that creates a stiff, cookie-cutter look. Choose skirts that are gathered, that have an extra yard of fabric for a richer appearance. In this instance, a cotton or wool jersey fabric that falls in loose folds is a good fabric choice.

Avoid straight skirts (also skimpy on fabric) and column-shaped dresses unless they have an excellent cut and flair. Remember your waistline!

When it comes to pants, exercise extreme caution. Now is the time to look for heavier fabrics— jersey is out: in pants, it will cling to every bulge. The all-American favorite, the pull-on polyester pant, is another fanny disaster.

If you must wear pants before your 30 days have passed, choose a sturdy denim or similar fabric. Denims don't have to be blue jeans—this solid fabric is available in all colors (yes, it's great in black). Team black denim pants with a crisp cotton shirt and a well-constructed jacket (don't forget the shoulder pads) for a great look.

Under it all. Your undergarments determine your finished look. Your bra must fit perfectly—no binding straps or too-small cups. A slip is a must under dresses and skirts for a smooth, bulge-free line. We have been liberated from most "support garments" (the very word *girdle* sends most women into a panic!), but one relatively new item is a great boon to slimness: control-top pantyhose. You get a smooth look from waistline to ankles and gone is v.p.l. (visible panty line). Wear them under everything, including pants!

Conquering the last fashion battle: swimwear. Here is where lycra comes in. In a one-piece suit with good internal construction, a lycra-blend fabric will firm and shape you like the best undergarment. As a cover-up, buy an oversized cotton scarf or shawl and tie it, sarong-style, just under your waistline. Watch the natives get restless!

6. Q&A

Q: Are vitamin supplements necessary?

A: The answer depends on the quality of your diet. If most of the foods you eat come from a jar, can, or box, you probably aren't getting the vitamins you need—supplements may be in order.

If you are following the Beautiful Bottom Diet and eating fresh foods, you have a better chance of getting nutrients naturally.

If you have any doubts, evaluate your overall health. If you're exercising, eating well, and getting the rest you need, yet still feel fatigued and run-down much of the time, then do consult a nutrition-conscious doctor about vitamin *and mineral* supplements.

Q: How can I prevent injuries?

A: First bear in mind than you are a lot less vulnerable to serious injury than you might think. Sitting without proper support at your desk all day can hurt your back more than any exercise you might do for a few minutes.

The Super Seven exercises are all safe, and there's certainly no danger in dancing. As an added precaution against sprains, be sure to warm up and cool down as suggested. And if you should ever feel a sudden or sharp pain, STOP, lie down and relax, then try again.

Be sure to follow the progression chart—don't rush to do Week 4's reps on your third day of exercising. That could cause soreness, and a reluctance to continue.

Q: When should I use ankle weights?

A: Once you've completed 60 days of exercising, you're ready for Advanced Level II, if you wish. Exercising with free weights (called "free" to distinguish them from machine-held weights such as Nautilus and Universal) increases your muscles' resistance, making them work harder and develop further. (You needn't worry about becoming muscle-bound—that would take *hours* of weight work a day.)

Free weights can be 5- or 10-pound dumbbells, heavy barbells for weight training, or weight cuffs that strap onto ankles and wrists. Perfect for the Super Seven, ankle weight cuffs of 2½ or 5 pounds really make the leg and seat muscles work. You can use the cuffs anytime—wearing them under pants while you're out walking is a great exercise bonus. Available at sporting goods stores, the cuffs should be demonstrated for you by a knowledgeable salesperson. Always ask questions and demand answers!

Q: Should I weigh-in every week?

A: The scale is a very unreliable tool for measuring your progress. Seeing a two-pound gain can be devastating—even if you know that it's just a temporary water weight gain. Another reason to avoid the scale is that a scale won't tell you how much of your weight is muscle, how much is fat, nor how much fat has been burned off versus how much muscle has been developed.

Muscle weighs more than fat, but has a smaller volume. Hence, the best way to measure your progress is with—you guessed it—your former nemesis, the tape measure.

With your determination, that bit of yellow fabric can become a treasured friend!

ABOUT THE AUTHORS

Deborah Cox is a top Ford model presently working in New York City. Previously she spent three years working in Europe for major designers and magazines. She has been seen in ads for L'Oreal, Clairol, Vassarette, and Cole of California as well as dozens of popular catalogs. Prior to starting her modelling career, she worked as a tutor for elementary school children.

Julie Davis is the author of twenty-five books, the first of which she wrote at age sixteen. Her nonfiction titles include five celebrity how-to's co-authored with singer Marie Osmond, model Beverly Johnson, actress Arlene Dahl, and two noted skin-care experts, Janet Sartin and Irma Shorell.